French crossword puzzles for kids with pictures to color

Educ Junior

EducJunior.com

This book is copyrighted.

All rights reserved.

Our information may not be copied in part or in full without our express written consent.

EducJunior.com

Version 1.00 2018

Table of Contents

Introduction   5

1   Puzzles   7

2   Solutions   41

Appendix   47

Introduction

Welcome to "**French crossword puzzles for kids with pictures to color**".

You'll find 32 crossword puzzles.
Each includes a grid that you must fill in with the letters of several French words to be discovered (four or five words depending on the puzzles).
Puzzles are organized per theme, indicated by the puzzle title on top of the page (in French and in English), all words to be found in a puzzle are related to this theme.
Words to guess are singular nouns..
To identify these words, instead of a definition like for classical crosswords, we use a picture which represents a word.

Here is an example of a picture and of the grid for the corresponding word:

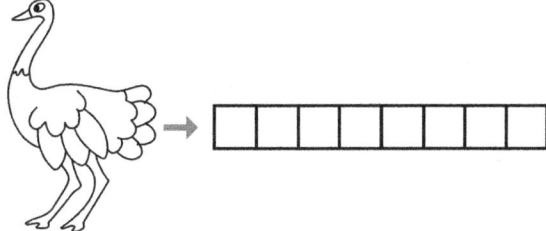

The picture represents an ostrich, "une autruche" in French, so we enter the capital letters AUTRUCHE in the grid, following the direction of the arrow originating from the picture:

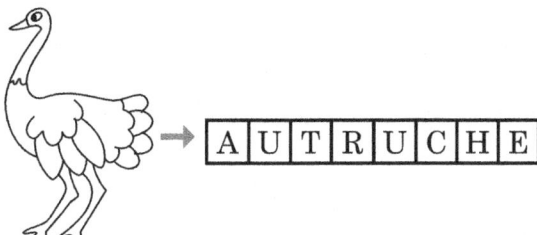

The following example has a grid with two words, one placed horizontally from left to right and the other placed vertically from top to bottom, these are the only two directions used for all puzzles:

To help to find the valid words, at the bottom of the puzzle page, in a smaller size, we include clues: the pictures and the first and last letters of the corresponding word.

Try to identify the words only with the main puzzle and look at the clues only if you are blocked.
At the end of the book, you'll find the solutions, the page number of the corresponding solution is shown at the top of the puzzle.
The solution comprises the completed grid and each picture with the associated word. Words are written in French with the English translation.

Here is the solution for the previous example:

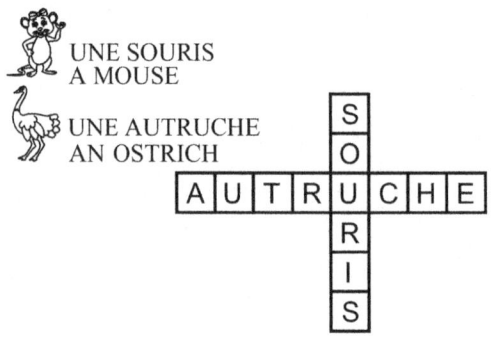

Grab a pencil and an eraser and start your first puzzle!

Once completed, color the pictures!

We advise you to use colored pencils and not felt-tip pens, to limit the risk of bleed through to the next page.

1
Puzzles

Puzzle 1
see the solution on page 42

Fruits
Fruits

Puzzle 2
see the solution on page 42

Animaux domestiques
Domestic animals

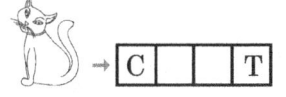 → C _ _ T  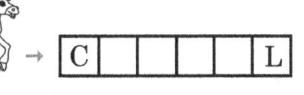 → C _ _ _ L  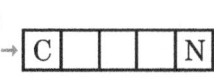 → C _ _ N 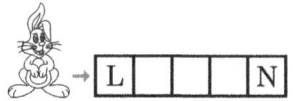 → L _ _ N

Puzzle 3

see the solution on page 42

Véhicules
Vehicles

Puzzle 4
see the solution on page 42

Petit déjeuner
Breakfast

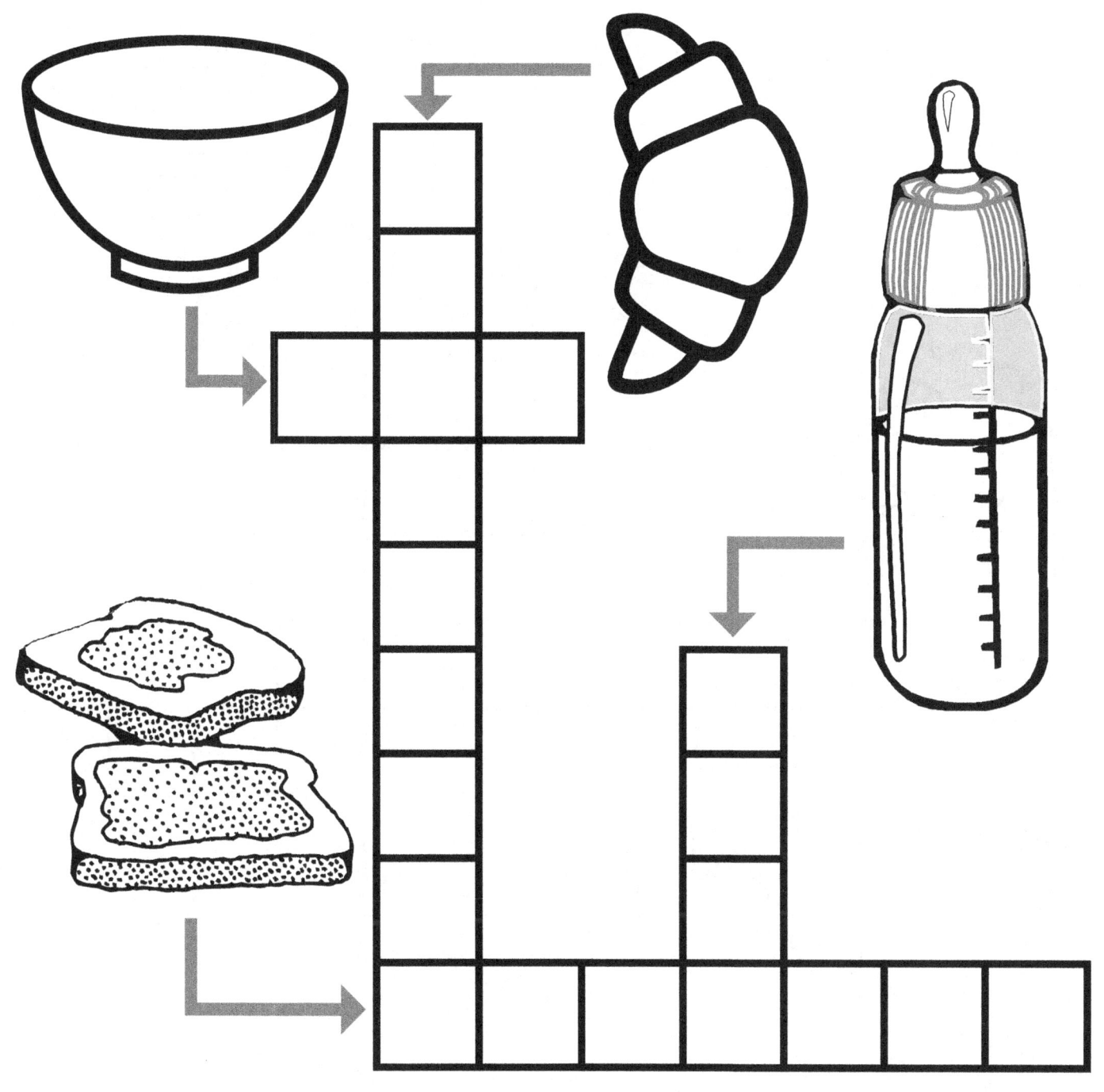

Puzzle 5
see the solution on page 42

À la ferme
At the farm

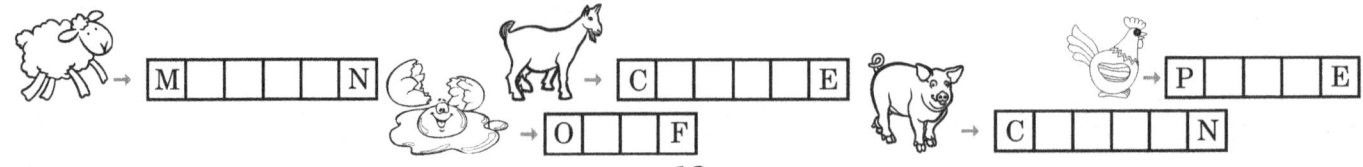

Puzzle 6
see the solution on page 42

À la plage
At the beach

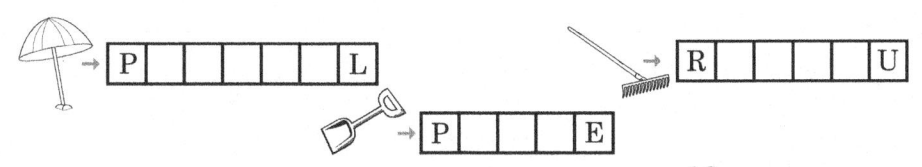

Puzzle 7

see the solution on page 42

Couverts
Tableware

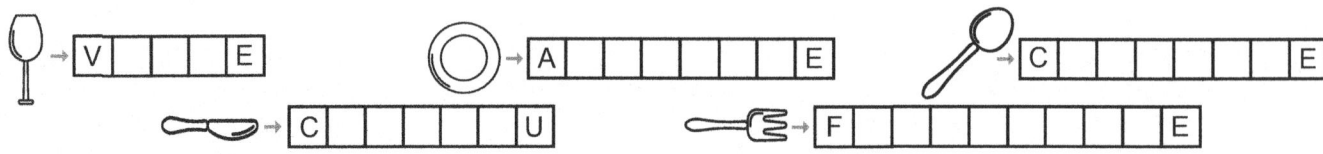

Puzzle 8
see the solution on page 42

Vêtements
Clothes

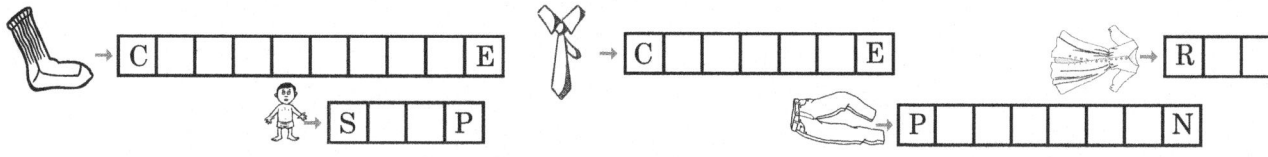

Puzzle 9
see the solution on page 43

Aliments
Food

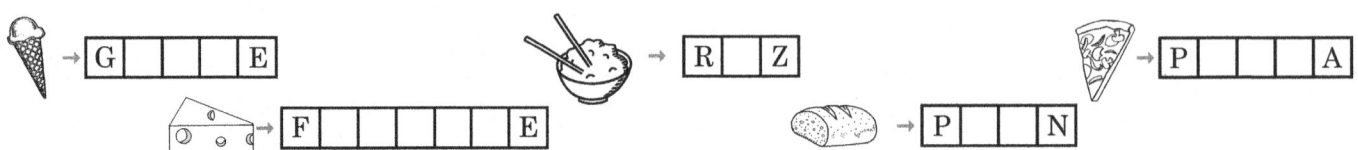

Puzzle 10
see the solution on page 43

Anniversaire
Birthday

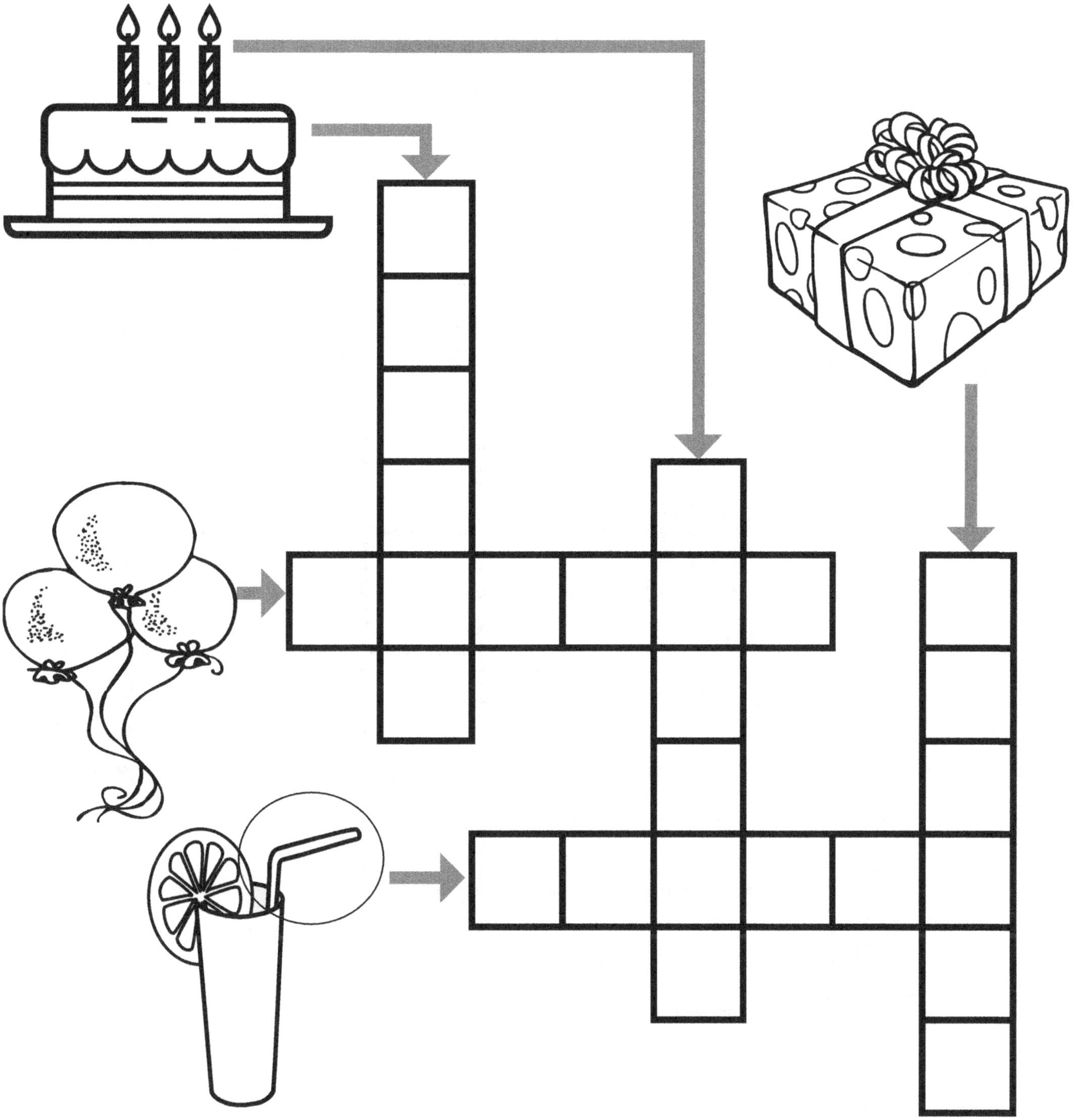

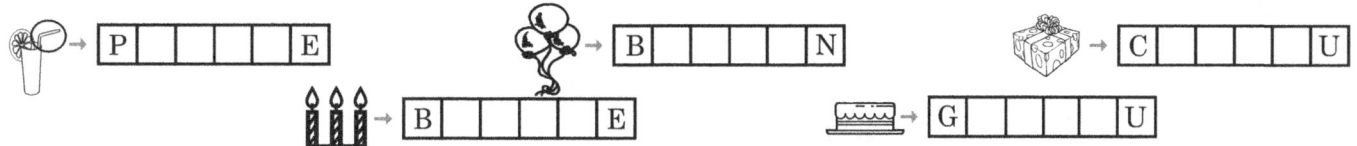

17

Puzzle 11
see the solution on page 43

Corps humain
Human body

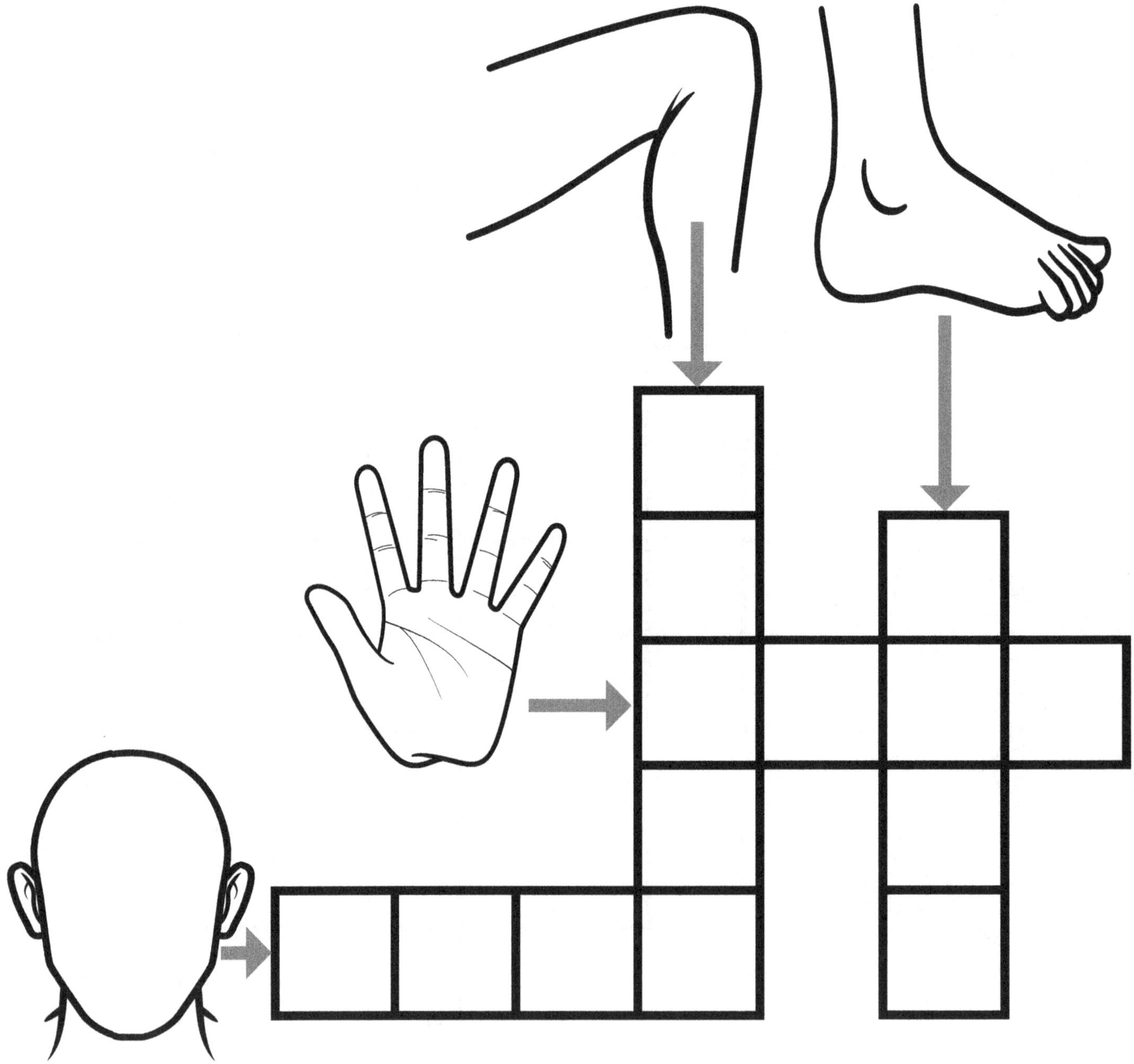

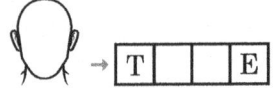 → T _ _ E

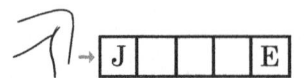 → J _ _ E

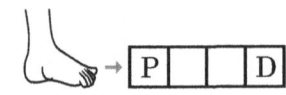 → P _ D

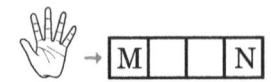 → M _ N

Puzzle 12
see the solution on page 43

Technologie
Technology

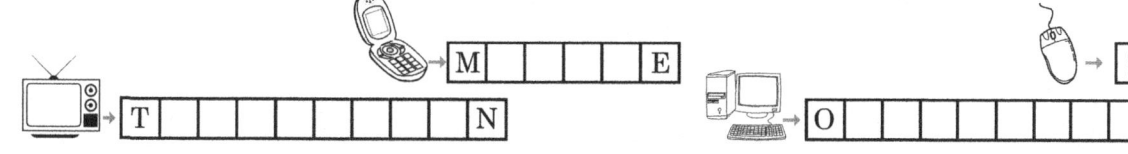

Puzzle 13
see the solution on page 43

Météo
Weather

☀ → | S | | L | ☂ → | P | | | | E | ☁ → | N | | | E | 🌧 → | P | | E |

20

Puzzle 14

see the solution on page 43

Fournitures scolaires

School supplies

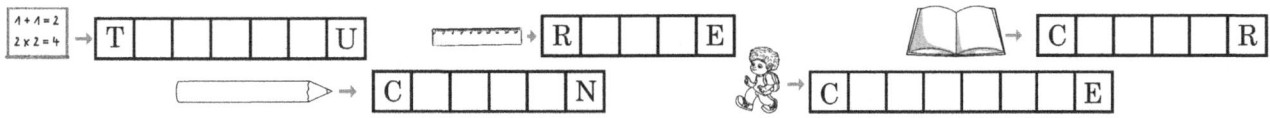

21

Puzzle 15

see the solution on page 43

Formes géométriques
Geometric shapes

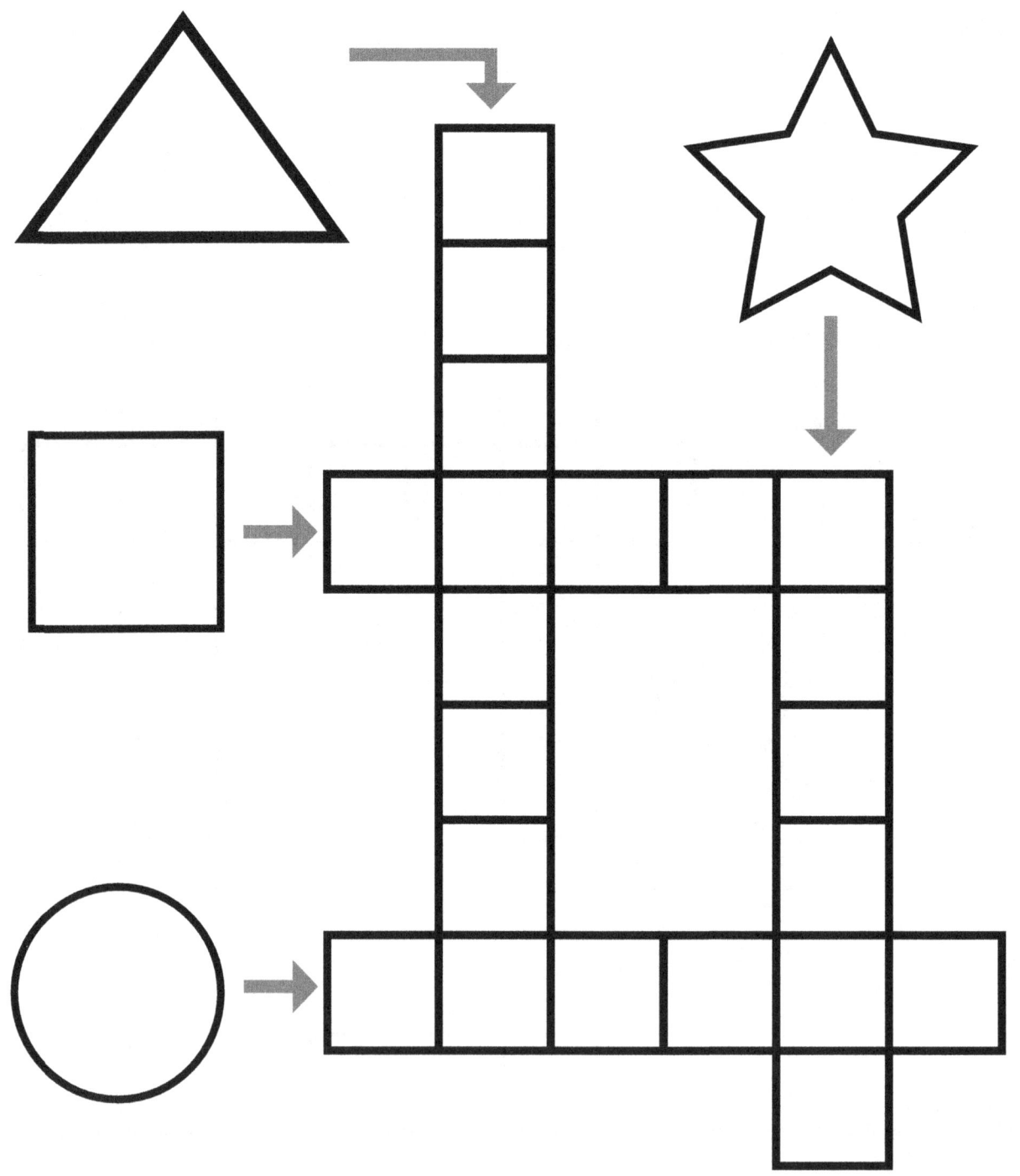

22

Puzzle 16
see the solution on page 43

Au cirque
At the circus

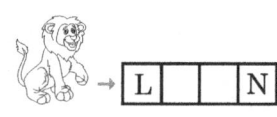 → J _ _ _ _ R

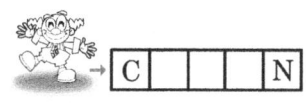 → L _ _ N

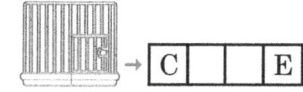 → C _ _ N

→ C _ _ E

Puzzle 17
see the solution on page 44

Animaux marins
Marine animals

24

Puzzle 18

see the solution on page 44

Bricolage
DIY

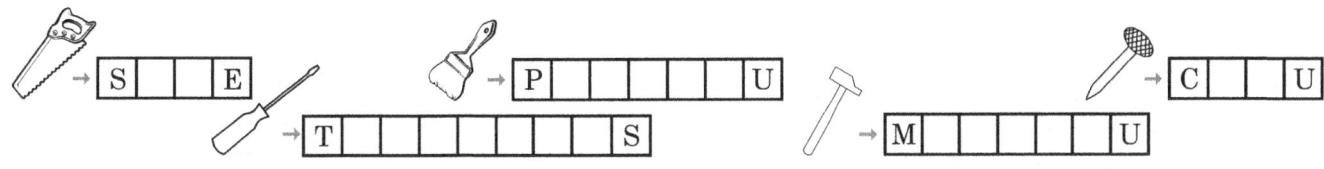

Puzzle 19

see the solution on page 44

Déguisements
Disguises

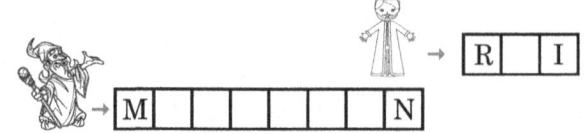

Puzzle 20

see the solution on page 44

Jeux
Games

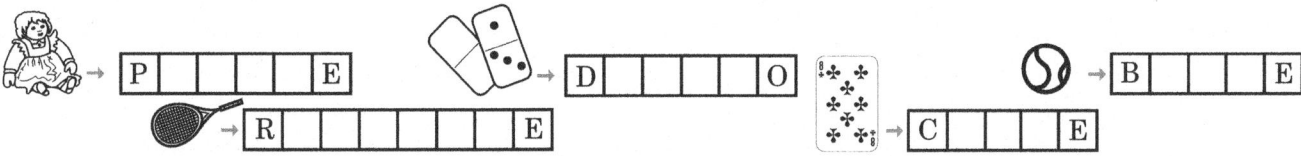

27

Puzzle 21
see the solution on page 44

Métiers
Occupations

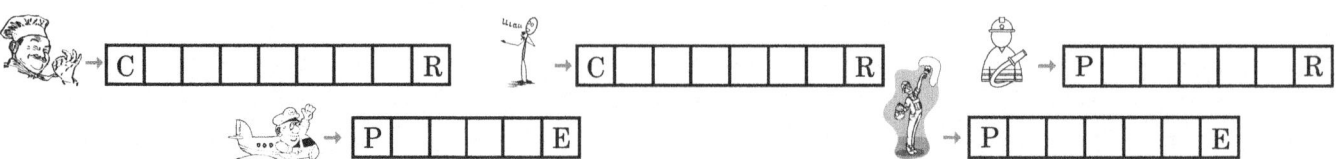

Puzzle 22
see the solution on page 44

Meubles
Furniture

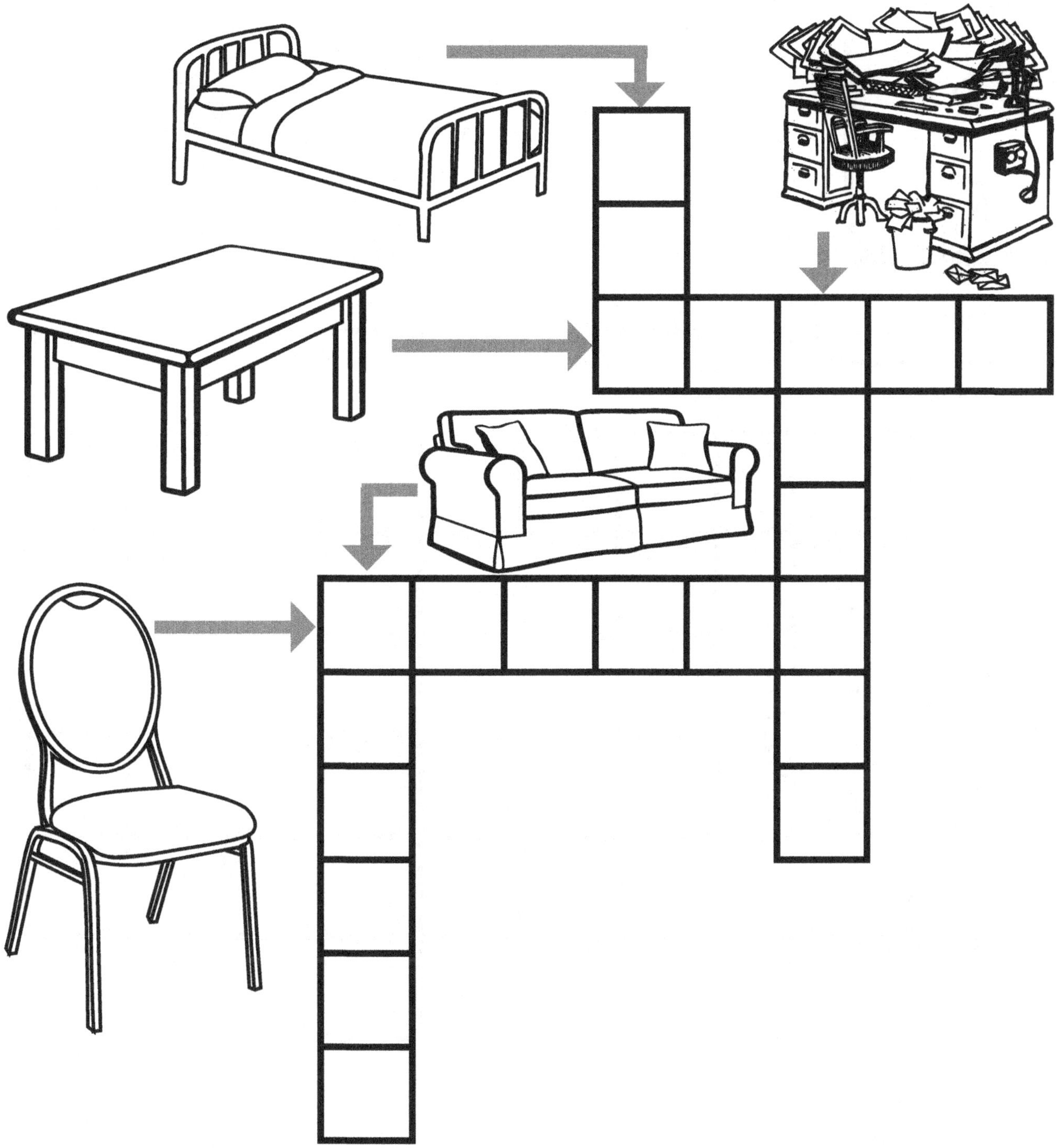

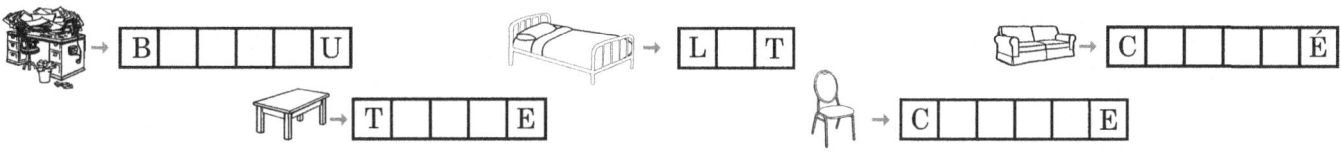

Puzzle 23

see the solution on page 44

Salle de bain
Bathroom

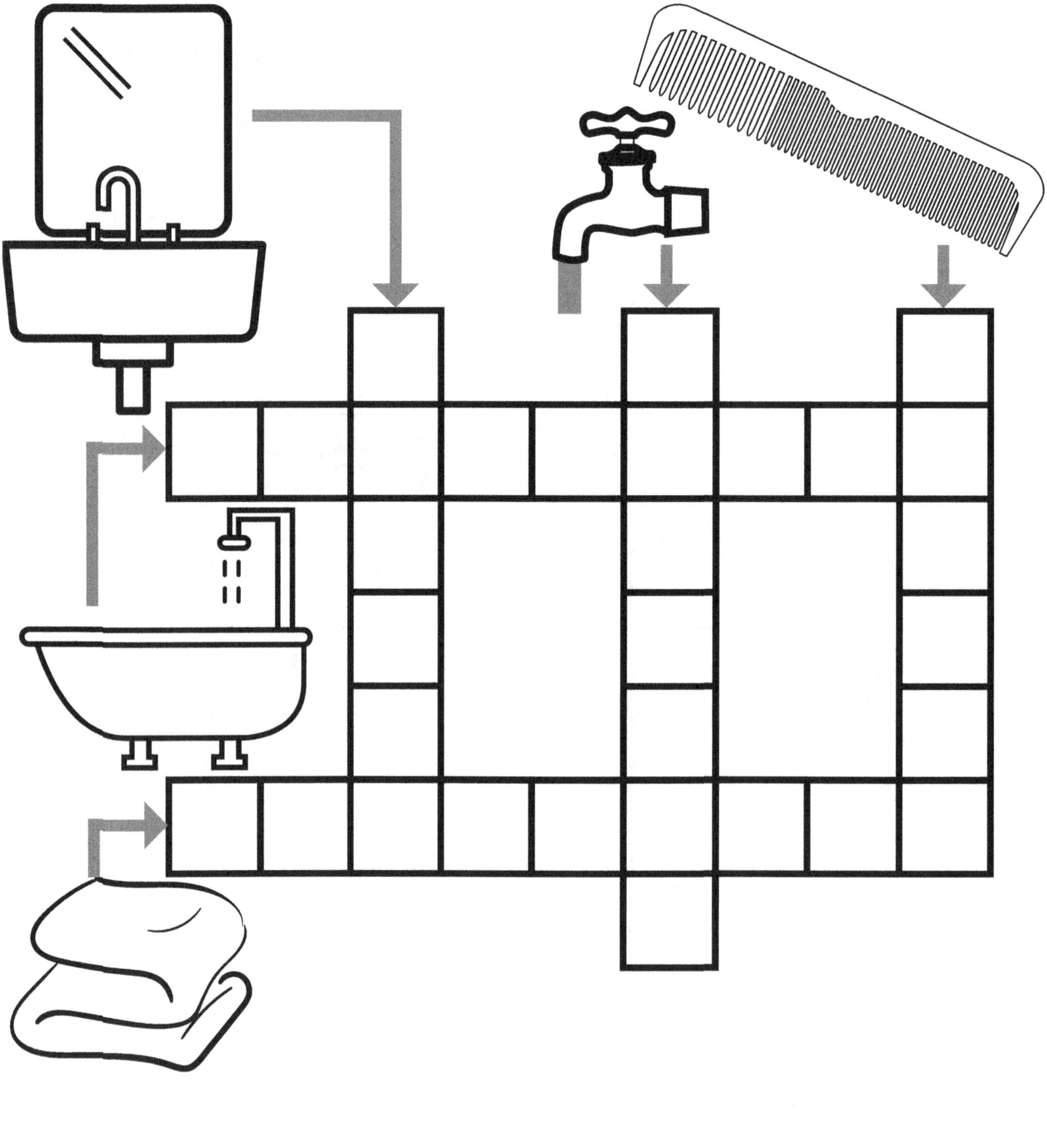

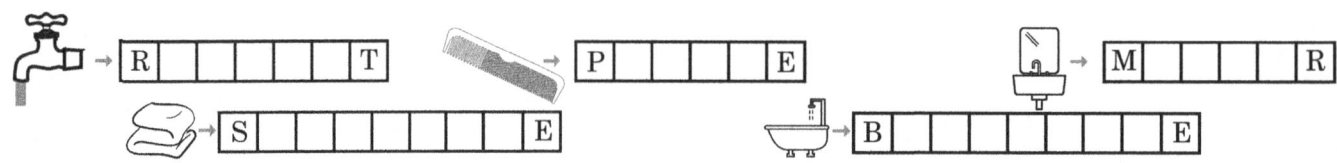

Puzzle 24
see the solution on page 44

Sports
Sports

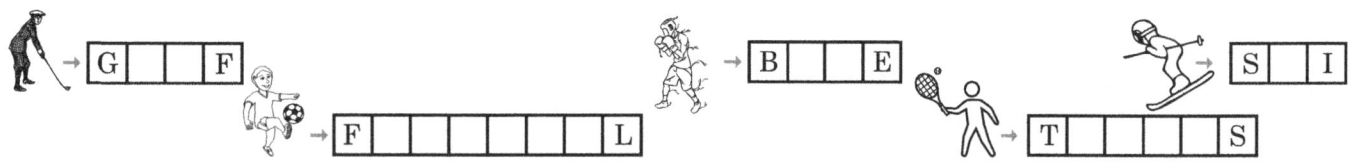

Puzzle 25
see the solution on page 45

Instruments de musique
Musical instruments

P O | T _ _ _ R | G _ _ _ _ E | V _ _ N

Puzzle 26
see the solution on page 45

Animaux de la jungle
Jungle animals

33

Puzzle 27
see the solution on page 45

Légumes et crudités
Vegetables

Puzzle 28
see the solution on page 45

Jardinage
Gardening

Puzzle 29
see the solution on page 45

Oiseaux
Birds

V _ _ _ R   P _ N _ _   A _ _ _ E   M _ _ _ U

Puzzle 30
see the solution on page 45

Armes
Arms

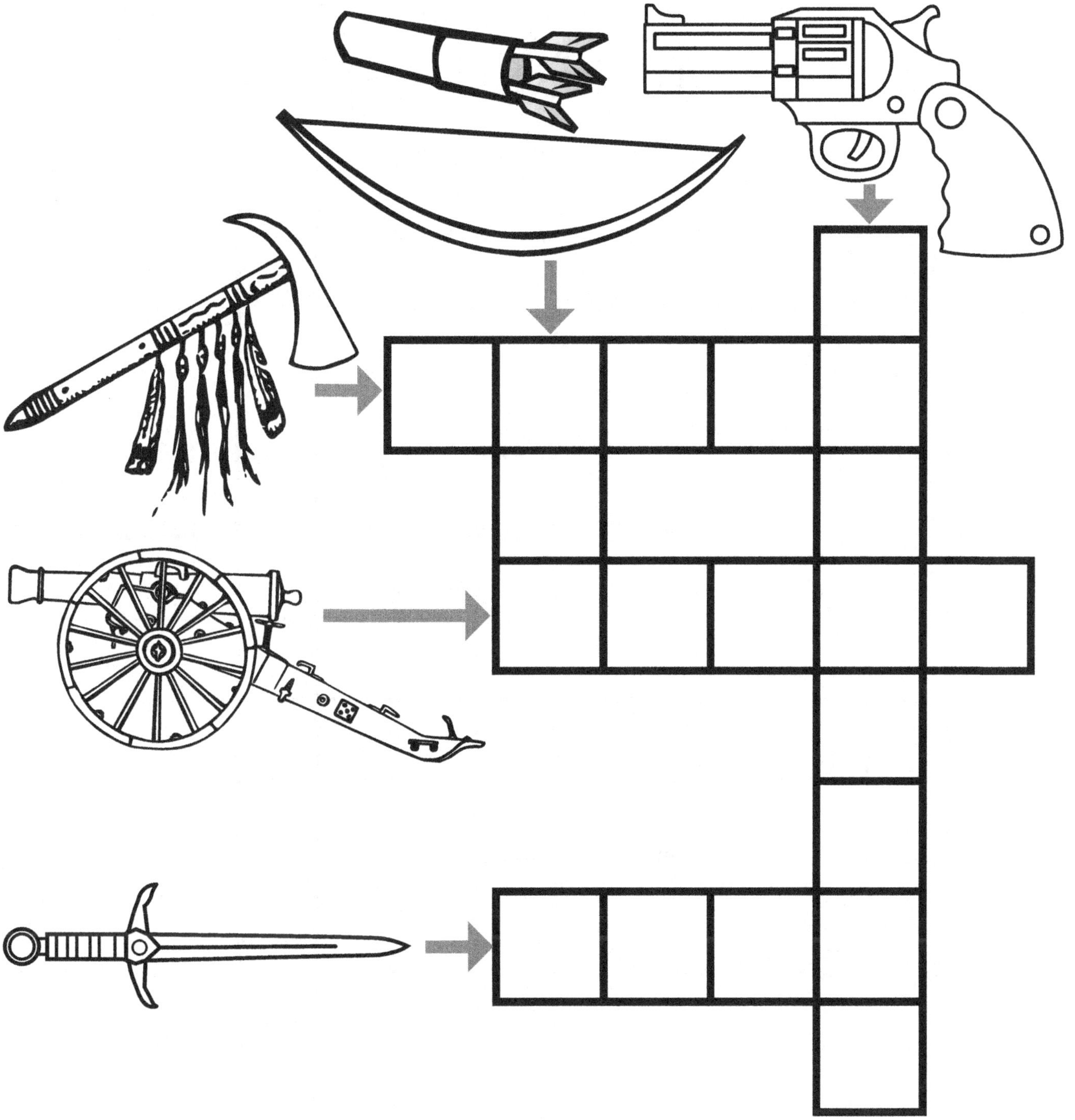

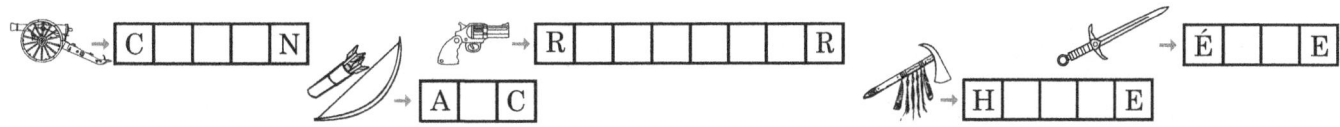

Puzzle 31

see the solution on page 45

Insectes
Insects

Puzzle 32
see the solution on page 45

Pirate
Pirate

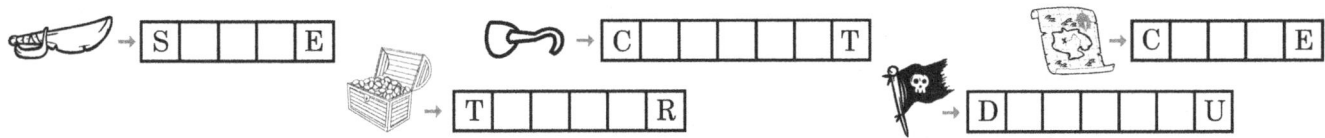

2
Solutions

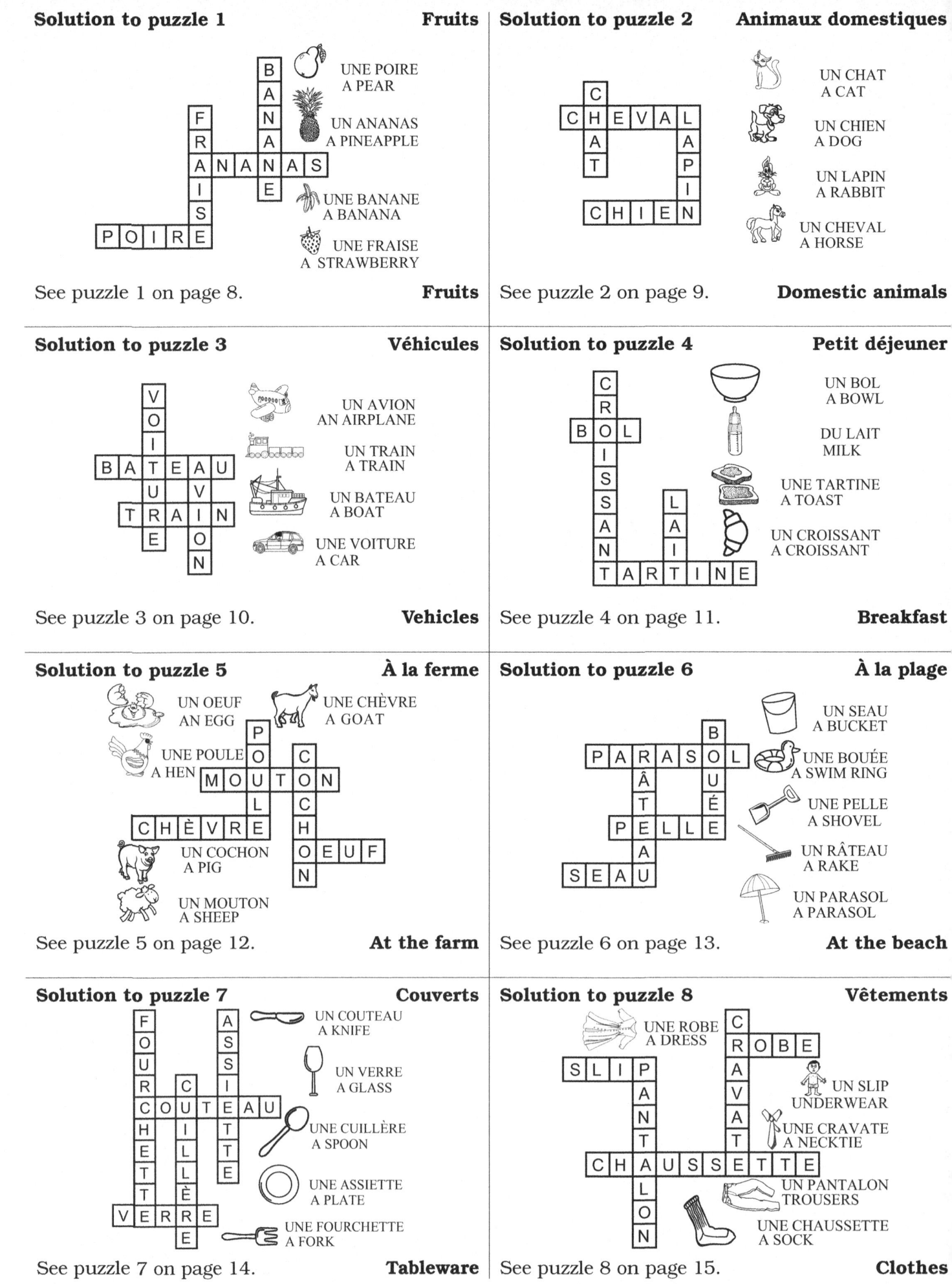

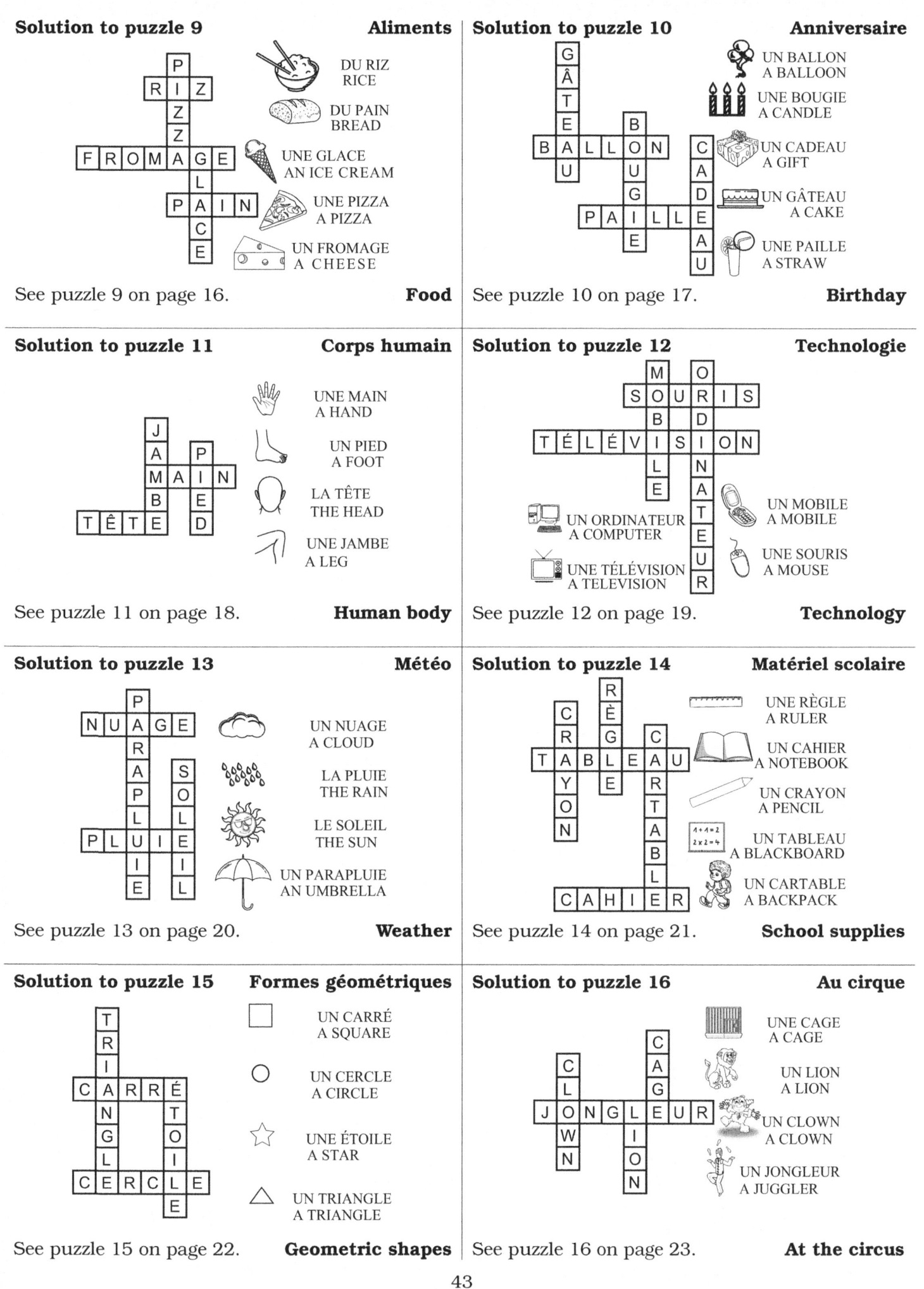

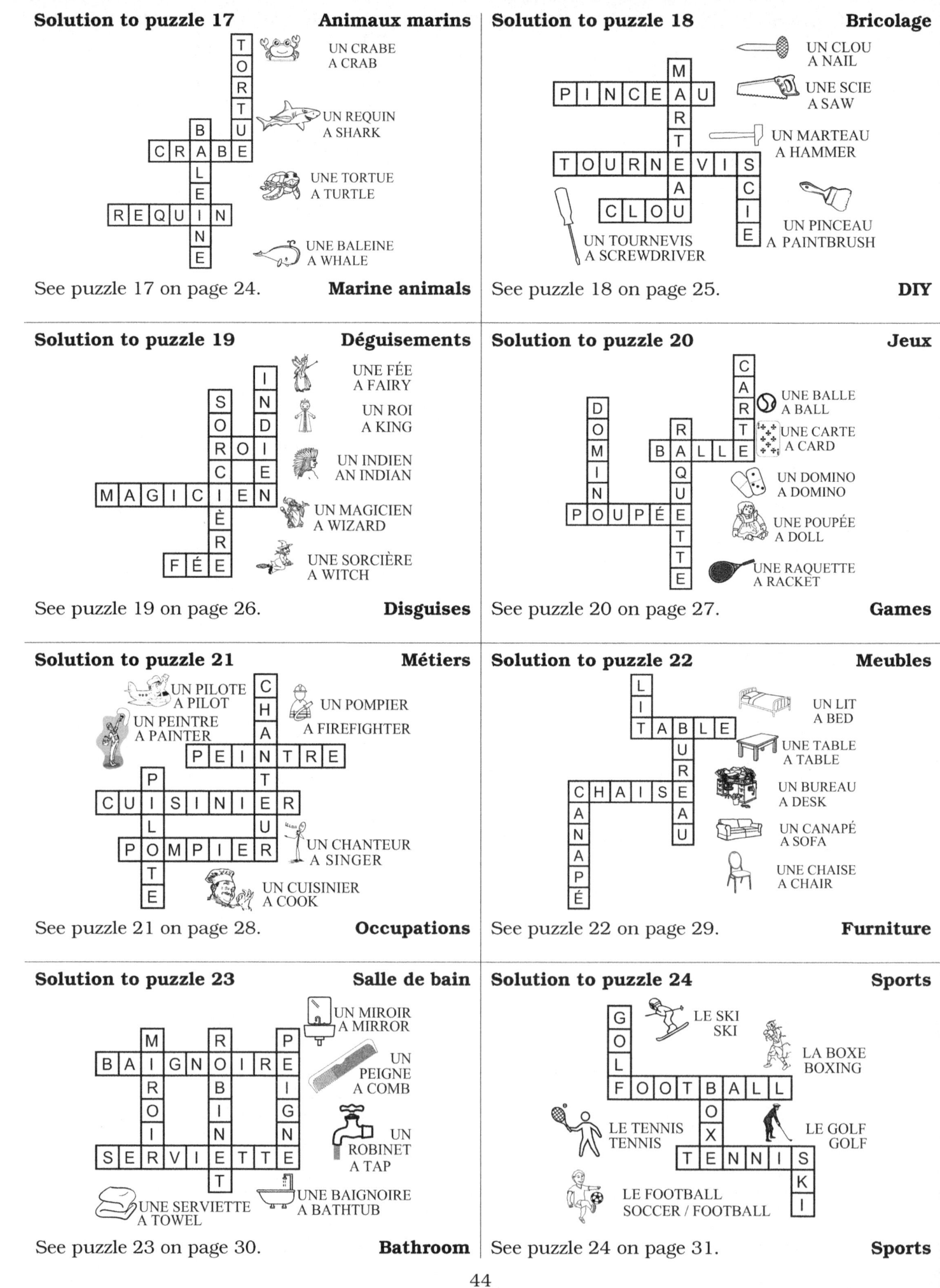

Solution to puzzle 25 Instruments de musique

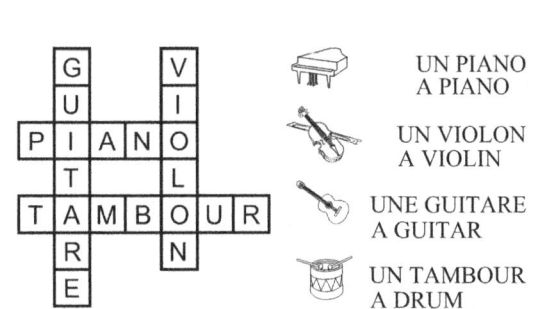

See puzzle 25 on page 32. **Musical instruments**

Solution to puzzle 26 Animaux de la jungle

See puzzle 26 on page 33. **Jungle animals**

Solution to puzzle 27 Légumes et crudités

See puzzle 27 on page 34. **Vegetables**

Solution to puzzle 28 Jardinage

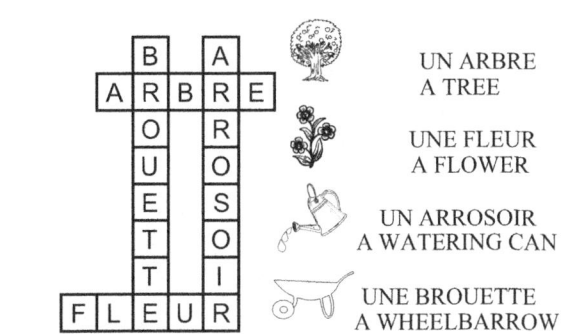

See puzzle 28 on page 35. **Gardening**

Solution to puzzle 29 Oiseaux

See puzzle 29 on page 36. **Birds**

Solution to puzzle 30 Armes

See puzzle 30 on page 37. **Arms**

Solution to puzzle 31 Insectes

See puzzle 31 on page 38. **Insects**

Solution to puzzle 32 Pirate

See puzzle 32 on page 39. **Pirate**

Appendix

Congratulations on finishing this book and completing all our puzzles.

If you are satisfied, thanks to write a short review on this book description page at Amazon's website.

And discover our other titles by clicking on the author's name, as several are planned.

Educ Junior

END.

Made in the USA
Monee, IL
18 November 2020